READ THIS FIRST!

Check out my FREE training on The Expert Showcase Series List Building Method

I would like to give you access to my video training here:

https://www.ExpertShowcaseSeries.com/video

This video training is a presentation of me teaching this method at a conference. It will help to visualize many of the concepts taught in the book as well as the accompanying workbook.

You will learn:

- How to get in touch with all the traffic you'll ever need even if you have no list
- Where to find people who already have lists and the 4 reasons why they will share traffic with you for free
- How to pre-qualify someone who has a list
- The truth about Joint Venture relationships and how using this exercise develops ongoing revenue with partners
- What to do if you have a challenging time with tech (HINT: my simple 2-page funnel will have people opt-in to your list)

Go check it now!
https://www.ExpertShowcaseSeries.com/video

TABLE OF CONTENTS

THE EXPERT SHOWCASE SERIES:

An Easy Way To Build Your List, Establish Partner Relationships and Grow Your Revenue

This book is designed to help you do three things:

- Build an engaged, enthusiastic email list
- Establish partner relationships that will serve both you and your partners in mutually beneficial ways, for years to come.
- Grow your revenue.

List building is near and dear to my heart—mostly because it's never *really* about "list building." Of course, I know that every new businessperson, bright-eyed with big dreams and full of potential, needs a list. So do well-established businesses. No matter where you find yourself—rookie, veteran or somewhere in between—list-building is a must.

But that list is so much more than just names and addresses inside of email-marketing software. When it's all said and done…

This is really about building *relationships*. It just so happens that list-growth is a byproduct of those relationships.

As a means toward helping you better achieve these ends, you'll also find *The Expert Showcase Series: 10 Day List Building Challenge Workbook*—a companion to this book, with actionable, easy-to-follow steps that will guide and help you track your progress as you build out your own expert showcase series within your market.

That said… let's talk about how to find your partners and build both relationships and the lists that come as a result. By doing so, you'll not only grow your business—you'll establish connection and authority within your market.

WHAT IS A RESPONSIVE LIST?

INTRODUCTION

Before we get into the bulk of my Expert Series Showcase method, I need to spend a bit of time discussing the basics of traffic.

When the topic of traffic comes up, it is always coupled with the question, "How do I get more traffic?"
I'll tell it to you straight—that is the wrong question. What you need to be asking is:

"How do I get the right kind of traffic?"

There are only three types of traffic:

1. Organic Traffic
2. Paid Traffic
3. Joint Venture Partner Traffic

The first two types of traffic have both advantages and disadvantages, but the third—Joint Venture Partner Traffic—has *no disadvantages whatsoever*.

Let's take a brief moment to talk about each of them.

ORGANIC TRAFFIC

Organic Traffic is traffic that is *naturally attractive* to the audience you want, based upon the assets you are offering.

For example, let's say we want to get traffic (people) to your landing page because it is there that you are offering something—an eBook, video, mini-course, etc.—in exchange for an email address (opt-in).

Over time, as we promote that landing page on the internet, it will gain more and more "authority" and a higher place among the ranks of search-engine visibility.

As this happens, your landing page is more likely to be seen when people are searching for the kind of subject matter that your work represents. The higher the result in a Google search, for instance, the more traffic your page receives, simply because of the reality that—whether they've heard of you or not—people are prone to click links given a higher place/result on that search engine (in other words: the first links available to them, in theory, represent the highest levels of authority on the subjects they search).

Without getting too into the weeds, *a ton* of work goes into getting your website/landing page/store/etc. better ranked among search engines. That process is called *Search Engine Optimization* (SEO), and is its own subject for another book entirely, so we're not going to talk about it here. What I want to discuss, simply, are the pros and cons of "organic traffic."

The greatest advantage that the organic approach offers us is called "*warm traffic*," which means: people were actively either searching for you, directly, or seeking answers to a specific problem/question/thought they had, and *boom!*—what you have to offer is *their* solution!

When this is the case, your email opt-in subscribers are described as warm, because you are the perfect match that they were looking for, and the likelihood of them becoming your customers—and purchasing any offer that you might present in order to help them solve their problem—increases. You have become their solution.

Make sense?

Organic traffic's disadvantage is that it takes time—and a lot of it. Moving up the search-engine ranks among millions of competing websites doesn't happen overnight, and the difficulty increases if your keywords, themselves, are competitive, because it makes it that much harder for people to find you. On average, you probably won't see any significant movement in your page's ranking for a good 90 to 120 days (and probably more). That aside, organic traffic is great traffic… if and when you can get it!

PAID TRAFFIC

Up next—paid traffic, which is also called *cold traffic*.

If *warm traffic* means that you're attracting people who are already looking for you, then *cold traffic* means that you're paying to get in front of an audience/market that is *not*. Rather, you are interrupting their "program"—blog, article, whatever it may be—with your ad/message.

For example: you are scrolling through Facebook when a video advertisement grabs your interest. You're not on Facebook to watch this video ad—you're on Facebook to post a picture of your breakfast and look at videos of your friend's dog chasing a frisbee.

Thus, the video is an interruption.

Now… it might be a *welcome* interruption. The person who sees your ad might watch it, like it, click it… even end up on your landing page and opt-in to your email list. But it's still cold traffic. It's nice that you have a new subscriber, but that new subscriber still 1) wasn't looking for you and 2) has no idea who you are.

The biggest advantage to this type of marketing is that paid traffic makes it possible to build a list extremely fast. You pay for ads, and the platform you pay disperses them to other users immediately. If your ads are compelling enough, the people who see them sign up for what you have to offer, and *voila*!—you're off to the races.

The *disadvantage*, though, is that—regardless of how pregnant your list is with possibility—the likelihood of turning your new *subscribers* into new and paying *customers* is a lot lower than it would be with a list full of warm addresses. To be clear, I'm not saying that paid traffic doesn't work at all, or that new subscribers *can't* be converted… only that this method isn't as strong a means of conversion, and your messaging had better be irresistibly compelling in order to sell to cold—albeit potential—customers.

JOINT VENTURE PARTNERS

The last and best type of traffic is that which comes from *Joint Venture Partners.*

This type of traffic comes from people who already have lists.

The people you contact with these lists would need to be willing to tell the people on their lists about you and your offer by directing them to click on a link, which would go to *your landing page*—mentioned in our previous examples—where the people on your Joint Venture Partners' list would then opt-in and subscribe to *your list.*

The advantage here—similar to that of organic traffic—is that this list is *warm.* It might even be better described as *hot,* because one of your partners, whom people already trust, is specifically recommending you to *their* list. In turn, they'll want to know more about you and what you have to offer, increasing the likelihood of a more responsive audience willing to purchase offers that you begin promoting to your new subscribers.

There are virtually *no disadvantages* to this type of marketing, and because of that, Joint Venture Partnerships are what we are going to be focusing on throughout this book.
Now that you understand traffic, I want to mention another term which really brings home the point of Joint Venture traffic and why it works so well…

Transfer of Authority

First of all, a quick story about this phenomenon.

In 2010, I attended a conference that focused on teaching people how to start an online business. That year, I was invited to participate as a guest-speaker, and given five minutes to present my topic:

How to build an online business while working a full time job.

The host wanted me to share my personal story. At the time, my days looked like this:

- Commute to work for 1.5 hours
- Work at the office for over eight hours
- Commute back home for another 1.5 hours
- Eat dinner with my wife and then-seven-year-old-twins
- Spend an hour with my kids, and put them to bed
- Spend the next five or six hours working on my online business
- Repeat

That routine lasted two years for me, and it took me six months to get my first client.

After those two years, though, my online business started to pick up speed, and I was able to leave my corporate job to work for myself full time.

It took me five minutes to tell over three-hundred people that story, and its purpose was simply to articulate a resonant scenario to others in the same position—to help *motivate* the conference's attendees to stick with it.

And then things got interesting.

When I stepped off stage, over thirty people crowded around to ask me more questions about my business. What was I doing? How was I doing it? How could they use my methods and apply them to *their* dreams?

To be honest, I didn't expect to become some sort of "expert" in the room, but it taught me—and I have continued to learn ever since—the power and value of the *Transfer of Authority phenomenon.*

You see, when the host invited me to speak from *his* stage—when *he* told them who I was and what I was going to speak about—his audience was able to trust me right away. I was vouched for as someone worth listening to. Our *host* called me trustworthy.

In short, he used his authority as host (who everyone else came to see) and transferred that authority (however brief, it was enough) to me.

For the rest of that weekend, people recognized and asked me questions. His transfer of authority even gave me the opportunity to take on consulting clients right then and there.

This same thing happens when you get leads from other people's lists.

They are the hosts—introducing you to their audience as someone worth trusting and paying attention to. In turn, their audiences will now see you as authoritative, as well. They will be more likely to click through to *YOUR* page, and opt in to *YOUR* list.

When that happens, you become the recipient of a warmer, more *RESPONSIVE* list, filled with people who will buy your offers because they know where they came from—the expert who recommended *you.*

Now that we've covered our bases, let's talk about The Expert Showcase Series, and exactly *how* to build your list, establish partner relationships and grow your revenue.

HOW TO GET PARTNERS IN YOUR MARKET TO SEND YOU SUBSCRIBERS

HOW TO GET PARTNERS IN YOUR MARKET TO SEND YOU SUBSCRIBERS

Let's start with a question:

How do you get partners in your market to send their subscribers to you?

Those of you who are familiar with my work already know this, but for those of you who are not: I love simple.

I love simple because it is both *effective* and *immediately actionable*. What this book describes—what I have to share with you—is simple. You can start implementing these principles and practices today. Right now.

This is based off of the Virtual Summit Model which is, in effect, a collaborative online event where experts in their respective field are interviewed by a host (that's you), specifically designed to generate leads from interested audiences.

I love this model. Virtual Summits are a great way to accomplish three important things:

1. A list-build
2. Generating relationships with the people you invite to participate
3. Revenue

The Virtual Summit Model is *effective*, but it's also a huge investment.

Although the idea is straightforward, online summits take time to organize. You have to schedule interviews with your guests. You have to make sure you've got the right tech (let alone internet connection) for live streaming your experts' interviews to your audience. You have to set up the course in a coherent way, organizing registrations and determining what you're going to offer during the process so that you can actually make money from your attendees…

It's a significant amount of work—and up to six months of it, on average. Usually, these summits are entirely *worth the work* put into them, but they do err toward all-consuming.

What I want to share with you today is called the Expert Showcase Series. It is simple, easy to implement, and every bit as effective as the Virtual Summit... but in half the time.

In fact, I've seen it done in less than thirty days.

That's why I love it.

For our purposes, here, I'm not going to focus much on revenue. While finalizing the sale is important, we're going to set it aside for the time being, because what I want to focus on is building relationships and building your list. After all, once that happens—and you've got a few hundred to a few thousand people (who trust you) on your list—revenue isn't a concern. In the words of everyone's favorite film narrator, James Earl Jones, *"If you build it, they will come."*

Well... that is... they *will* come, if you have the list to drive them there.

Using this model, you can get to those few hundred to a few thousand numbers pretty quickly, and then begin an offer campaign for expedited revenue streams instead of wading through the six-month process of preparing an online summit.

How does this work?

It's enough for people in someone's audience to get excited about new content being released from their favorite expert. But imagine ten experts whose new content is being released as an authoritative stamp on your market's interests...

Now, imagine that all of these experts share what they're doing with their lists. It's safe to assume that their audience will care about what they have to say, which stands to suggest that they'll also care about what you're doing (plus, in all likelihood, your experts' lists contain other experts whose lists contain other experts... so the interest grows exponentially). At the very least, you've just become the funnel that people must pass through in order to access your guests' content.

Your experts let their audiences know that they're being interviewed with these other experts, and in order for people to see these interviews, they must now opt into your list...

Which is exactly what you're doing when you pre-register (or construct the pre-registration process) for an Online Virtual Summit. Suddenly, a series of otherwise disconnected interviews have become an exciting event!

For most summits, though, people usually have to pay something (or, at least, *decline an ask*) in order to access the promoted content. In this case, though, the "paywall" is… an email address.

A simple opt-in form gives everyone access to multiple, leading experts' insight, wisdom and guidance within your market. At that point, the choice becomes a given: with value like that and no financials required, *of course* your Expert Showcase Series is worth subscribing for!

So, let's build your Field of Dreams…

Step One: Find the partners in your market.

We're all in different markets, but the method is universal. How do we find the "right" partners or experts in each of our respective fields?

Quite simply: *utilize social media.*

You don't know it yet, but everyone you need to talk to is on Google, Twitter, Instagram, YouTube, Facebook, Amazon or [insert your favorite follower platform here] search away.

When I started teaching this material years ago, none of these resources were as accessible as they are today. Facebook wasn't thriving the way that it has in recent years. Instagram was only a recent Facebook acquisition. Pinterest promotions were nonexistent or underutilized. There was no such thing as influencer marketing as we know it.

But we know it now.

Today, all we have to do is pick an avenue—Google, Facebook, Amazon, you name it—to find partners a couple of clicks away. So… where are yours? In the coming chapters, I'll tell you exactly where they are, and *exactly* how to find them.

In addition, my *Expert Showcase Series: 10 Day List Building Challenge Workbook* will give you an even greater, more in-depth step-by-step guide to follow along with as we work through this material together.

Step Two: Ask for an interview.

When you find experts in your market, you're going to simply ask them for an interview. Sound familiar? It should—this is not too dissimilar from the online summit…

But my way is easier. I'm not asking you to prepare an hour's worth of questions, and you don't have to become a professional *question-asker* (or experience the intimidation that comes from having to keep your guest—not to mention your listeners—engaged for the entire conversation).

I want you to ask your experts one question. Just one. We'll get to *what* that question should be momentarily, but first…

Step Three: Set up a simple, two-page funnel.

Without step three, we have no way to collect email addresses for our list-build, and no way to showcase our expert interviews to interested subscribers.

This step involves a bit of tech-work to complete, which I know can be daunting for some people. Don't worry! Speaking of experts—you don't have to be one in order to easily capture a professional-quality interview with your guests. I'll show you *exactly* how to do it.

Before we move on… I'd like us to ask ourselves a question, as well:

Why?

Why would the experts that you find want to partner with you? Why would they agree to an interview with you? Why would they want to participate in your efforts? After all… have they ever heard of you before? Are you even in *their* market? *Who are you?*

I'll give you four reasons:

1. *Ego.*

Plain and simple. Experts have egos, just like all of us. More often than not, you'll receive a "yes" simply because they like being liked. Why do you think Facebook does so well? People like being liked. They like being included.

I'm not saying you won't hear the word "no." You will. I'm not saying you won't get ghosted, either. Plenty of people will not respond to your emails. But plenty of people will.

2. *Content.*

Content is funny. Everybody wants to produce content… except for experts. Experts exist in their own universe. They're great at what they do, but they're not always great at letting others in on the fact that they do it.

Stephen King is a phenomenal writer. The King of Horror. He has conquered his genre, right? But maybe he's not the King of Facebook Posts, or the King of the Blogosphere. (Who knows? I'm making it up.) His readership is global, and he wants to keep writing *what he is good at*. Someone else is putting the content together, and though that person may not be the writing expert that King is, his or her work is still a valuable necessity that supports King's livelihood.

The point is: you'll often find that experts don't want to put out their own content, so…

You're going to put it out for them.

And you're going to tell them so. It's a free, valuable piece of content that you are going to share with your list so that they can see this interview *with them*.

3. *The One Question (and the Expedited Process).*

When it comes to your guest experts' reasoning and participation, simplicity is powerful, and their time-investment is short. Put bluntly: an expert doesn't want to be on a call with you for an hour. But if you only need *ten minutes* of their time for one question? That changes the game.

What is your one question going to be? Perhaps it is an aspirational question. Perhaps it is a problem-solving question. Perhaps it is both. For example:

"What are the best business strategies that you are using with your clients today?"

If you ask ten leading experts in your particular industry what their best client strategies are, wouldn't everyone—on all of their lists—want to hear what that expert and all those other experts have to say about all those strategies?

Of course they would.

What we want to do is cut the process in half so that every step is easier, and the likelihood of receiving your "yes" is assured.

4.   *FOMO.*

Good ol' FOMO. Plain and simple. *The Fear Of Missing Out.*

Here's the reality: when you first invite your soon-to-be "partners" to participate in your event, some will say yes, and some will say no, and others won't respond at all. Once you've got a few yeses in the bag, you can easily follow up with the no's, and with those experts who haven't yet responded to your request, and let them know about those who have...

Enter: FOMO.

"Woah! If Stephen King said 'Yes' to this interview, I definitely should, too!"

You'll see no become yes, and—like magic—non-responders will suddenly remember how to hit "reply" on an email, agreeing to your interview.

[One quick note before we move forward: regarding FOMO, don't get paralyzed thinking that you've got to find celebrity-status experts. Successful list building isn't predicated upon "A-List" guests. What we're really looking for is not so much whether our experts have public notoriety, but whether they've got the kind of lists that make for successful collaboration.]

Following me? Good.

LET'S GET STARTED

When setting out to find your experts, start with a simple Google search.

For example, I'm going to use the yoga market, but the point is to take whatever market you are in and type something like, "top experts in [your niche/market]."

So, I type out "top experts in yoga" and Google gives me pages upon pages of different experts in the yoga world. The list of "experts" is practically never-ending, but you're looking for something specific.

In order to "prequalify" who, among these infinite market-leaders, you should reach out to, you'll want to click on their websites and look for one thing, in particular:

An opt-in box.

If you go to a website and they're not—at the very least—collecting email addresses, then you know they're not doing a good job of marketing themselves. It's that plain, and that simple.

If they have an opt-in box, then chances are, they're building a list. That is your prequalification. (Even better if their opt-in box is above the fold, because chances are, that list is important to the expert, and the people on that list are paying attention).

As you'll discover, Google will give you a list of fifty to one-hundred potential interviewees right off the bat, but let's take it a step further...

Let's move to Facebook.

On Facebook, we'll conduct a similar search. In my example: yoga. That's the market. And just like Google, the social media giant will spit out a list of hundreds of people involved in yoga.

Here, though, we're going to focus our attention on Facebook Pages. When you click the Pages header, you'll find the top Pages in your market, which will not only reveal who Facebook's top experts are in your field, but how many people follow them.

Yes, we're looking for Likes on Facebook Pages. Look for the ones with thousands. Tens of thousands. In "yoga," I found a few with millions of Likes.

Message them in the same way that you would otherwise email them. Tell them that you want to interview them.

Finally, let's talk about Amazon.

What is Amazon really good at, besides e-commerce products? Where did they start?

Books.

And who writes books?

Experts.

So what are we going to do?

Search for books written by experts in our market.

When I type the word yoga into my search bar, Amazon's algorithm gives me a list of books that might be of interest. When I scroll down, I'll see another list—on the left-hand side of my screen—that says, "Authors." When I click it, Amazon will give me a list of all of the authors who have written books on my subject. Furthermore, it will tell me (in parenthesis beside their names) how many books each author has written, which will help me screen out who I'm looking for because—theoretically, anyhow—the more books written equals the more work done and expert advice available in my market.

You can also cross-reference each person's online presence to make sure that they're on top of their game (read: worth reaching out to). Sure, an Amazon search may wield an "expert" with fourteen books beneath his belt, but what's his website like? Does he/she have the opt-in form essential to your list-building plans, or is his site an expired GoDaddy page (and, of those fourteen books, how many of them are actually about yoga, vs. children's books he thought might be fun to release for his nephews)?

Do your homework, of course, but these examples should get you 100 experts worth contacting right away, And you can repeat these steps wherever you'd like to. LinkedIn. Twitter. Pinterest. Instagram. YouTube. You name it. Anywhere there is an influencer in your market that's a good place to search.

WANT YOUR EXPERTS TO BE SO EXCITED THAT THEY CAN'T WAIT TO POINT THEIR LISTS TO YOU? HERE'S EXACTLY WHAT TO DO

WANT YOUR EXPERTS TO BE SO EXCITED THAT THEY CAN'T WAIT TO POINT THEIR LISTS TO YOU? HERE'S EXACTLY WHAT TO DO

If we're going to invite our newfound experts to an interview, we're going to need copy.

We need messaging.

In this book, I've written the introductory email copy for you, specific to each platform we'll be taking a look at together. All each needs is a touch of personalization. It's important that we get this right, because each of our resources functions uniquely. Email copy is one thing. Facebook and Twitter copy are another.

For example, let's take a look at our email process, beginning with two simple steps:

1. Send an interview request.
2. Confirm with those who have said yes, and send a follow up request to those who have said no or haven't yet responded.

When the time nears to begin promotion, you'll want to send your experts another couple of emails, letting them know that your series is ready, and that they can promote it, too.

Here, it is important to make swipe copy available to your experts. The reason is twofold: we want to assure ourselves of correct messaging, and we want to eliminate any additional work (read: roadblocks) that might deter your expert guests from participating in your promotion.

I want to go through one particular piece of copy so that you understand the mental triggers used to help the experts easily say yes to the interview.

Let's take a look at the email you would use to invite your experts to be interviewed.

Below, I have provided the copy itself, as well as a few notes—*[italicized, bracketed and indented to help you differentiate between the two]*—to help you understand key points along the way.

This is for someone in the health and wellness market.

Here's the invitation:

SUBJECT:

I'm putting together an expert showcase. Can I feature you?

BODY COPY:

I'm putting together a showcase of selected well known people in the health and wellness space. It's called The Health & Wellness Expert Showcase. I thought you'd be perfect for it.

All I would need is 10 minutes of your time.

[Right there. 10 minutes].

I'll help spread the word about you and your business to thousands of people and drive a ton of new subscribers to your list.

Is that something you'd be interested in?

Here's a little bit more about what I'm putting together...

My goal is to interview between 15 and 20 industry experts and have them give their best piece of advice in 10 minutes or less.

Here's a partial list of people I've invited to participate so far.

[List those experts. And what's important here is that he said, "I've invited." Keyword: invited. And he lists all the people that he invited. So you're gonna do the same thing.]

Here's **what's in it for you…**

Once I've interviewed everyone, I'll be releasing them all at once free on one page. Right underneath your video, I'm going to include a link to your site driving traffic to your list, or to any other offer you'd like to promote -the choice is yours.

[This paragraph is important, too. I told you this isn't a revenue generating event, but it can generate revenue because if you put a link under each one of their videos, that links back to their opt-in form to their website to maybe one of their courses. Those links could be affiliate links. So as these people are watching the expert series, they like a particular expert, they click on it, they want to buy from them. You can get a percentage of that just by putting that link there. I don't focus on it, but I definitely have seen a lot of people make money by just doing that. So I wanted to point that out to you.]

I'm also going to do a big launch campaign to get your content in front of even more people, and even give some experts to offer the summit page as an added bonus to their products.

I'm going to do everything I can to make sure everyone who participates gets as much traffic and exposure as possible.

All I need from you right now is to let me know you're in.

(Just hit reply and say "I'm in!" and I'll get you more details.)

> *[Again, making it super easy for them just hit reply and just say I'm in. That's it. They don't have to fill anything out.]*

I'll schedule a 10-minute interview with you that fits around your schedule, of course.

I'm going to be asking you this question:

What's your number one strategy that's working really well for you and your clients to achieve their health and wellness goals?

Once I have that, I'll just need the link to your website or opt in page.

The only other thing I'll ask is that you also promote this summit to your own list. Once it's live. I'll give you all the copy you need which you can choose to edit or send as is whichever is easier for you.

So, can I count you in?

[YOUR NAME]

P.S. Is there anyone else you know who would be a good fit for this as well? If, so please let me know. Thanks!

> *[You're asking for a referral. That happens all the time. They're like, yep, you know who else would be good for your series? So and So. And then also here, making sure that you tell them that part of this process is that they promote it to their list once it's live.]*

This is the starting email. This is how we're going to get people to respond to you. You'll get yeses right away… and you'll get no's… and you'll get people who don't respond at all.

Once you've begun to receive your yes from people, you're going to write a follow up email to the folks who either haven't responded, or have already said no, saying, "Here are the people who are participating."

Then, you're going to list who they are. And that's when the FOMO kicks in.

RELATIONSHIPS

RELATIONSHIPS

The Expert Showcase Series works. Here's what a salesperson in the Real Estate market had to say after implementing my model:

I wanted to share a big win for me this week. On Marc Evans' recommendation, I started an interview series for real estate investors called "Real Estate Investing Rock Stars." On Monday, I emailed everyone whose contact info I could find. Today, I am proud to say that I have landed some of the biggest names in my industry—Than Merrill of Fortune Builders, and Ron Legrand! In the Real Estate investing business, this is HUGE!

I have twelve experts so far, am well on my way to twenty, and—at this rate—expect to have much more than that!

It is exciting when you receive your yes from people willing to participate in your interviews. Once you do—coming full circle—it's time to start building relationships.

Let's talk about the crux of this method.

The interview acts as the start of your relationship-building. It is also the place where you'll notice the strategic byproducts that come as a result of your efforts. Perhaps your interviewees will even begin to reciprocate with offers for you.

"Hey, why don't we do this together?"

"Hey, why don't we do that together?"

You're developing a relationship.

One of the best aspects of this process is that you're not asking these experts to go buy your stuff. You're asking them to be interviewed.

It's an entirely non-invasive way to get your foot in the door.

Now, imagine this scenario: you go through the whole series with ten to twenty experts. They're happy with the traffic that's being redirected to their sites, and you're building your list…

What happens next? Who knows where the opportunities might lead?

Perhaps you've developed a product or service, and your offer is ready to go. You want to invite your newfound partners into a business relationship and/or a profit share. How easy is it—at this point—to go back to them and say, *"Hey, remember when we did that list building exercise, and I interviewed you? Well, I'm selling this course now, would you like to hear about a business opportunity on how we could share profits together?"*

You think they'd be open to hearing what you have to say, especially now that you have an established relationship, and your entire history hasn't consisted of beating down their door with salesy pitches from the get-go?

This is how businesses get built—off of these relationships. List building is a part of it, sure, but it is relationships that will continuously grow your business.

Another great thing about this model is its replicability.

Do it once, repeat. Do it twice, repeat.

After you've found ten to twenty people, you can find ten to twenty more, compounding your value, adding experts exponentially and funneling your traffic to a space where your authority is firmly established. Through it all, the incentive to participate in your offer grows, the number of relationships that you have an opportunity to invest in grows and—of course… your list grows.

HOW TO SET UP A SIMPLE 2-PAGE FUNNEL TO PROMOTE YOUR PARTNER SERIES

HOW TO SET UP A SIMPLE 2-PAGE FUNNEL TO PROMOTE YOUR PARTNER SERIES

The final piece in our puzzle is the *two page* funnel, which is exactly how it sounds:

- Page one: an opt-in form
- Page two: all of the embedded interviews

That's it.

You can create a two-page funnel on your own, or using templates in ClickFunnels, Kajabi, LeadPages, Wordpress… wherever.

On the first page, create an opt-in form. There's a place for a logo, there's a place for a picture or video headline on the right, a place to put your email address, and some other copy underneath.

On the second page is the Expert Series. You can embed both your video and a pretty cover-photo of your participants for each, which new subscribers will simply click to view. Beneath each expert video, you can include their name, a short quote or blurb and—if applicable—a hyperlink back to their website, or their own opt-in form, or an affiliate product.

Here is an example of what this looks like from Kristal, who I worked with in the Healing the Body market.

In the first picture (left side), you can see her opt-in form, which asks the question:

What is the single greatest contributor to healing the body?

This form is the target page that all of her experts linked to when they emailed their lists about their participation, and every one of their subscribers was required to sign up for her list in order to see the Expert Series answers to that question.

Once the site visitor has subscribed by opting in to Kristal's list, they receive access to the expert interviews (right side).

It's that simple.

I've used this Expert Series model with clients in nearly every market imaginable, but just in case you're wondering whether or not it will work in yours.. it will.

I know it will, because it is time-tested, experiential and proven. Over and over again—even as far back as when I taught this material in relation to an eBook (as opposed to a video series)—it has worked.

In fact, at one of my live workshops, a man named Douglas approached me during our break to say, "Marc, I did your old list building process. And I have over *4000 people that signed up from doing your exercise.*"

At the time, that exercise was building this as an eBook, instead of the video series that I'm showing you now. For what it's worth, though, eBooks still work today. This is simply an updated model. In general, I think that video will prove to be easier for you and your expert guests, and better for your audience, as people are far more engaged in visual content. Either way, Douglas got about 4000 signups.

This *will* work in every market.

Admittedly—in the beginning—I wasn't sure I could say that. Now that I've seen it for myself, I am. My confidence is based upon experience, and I'll wrap this up by telling you a story about it...

THE
IMPOSSIBLE
MARKET

THE ~~IM~~POSSIBLE MARKET

Leanne was in the NICU market (essentially: a hospital for premature babies, or babies that have some form of concerning condition when they are born).

When Leanne approached me with the hope of implementing my Expert Series model in her space, I had my doubts...

but I also had a vested interest in trying.

I have twins. They were born prematurely and spent thirty days in the NICU before I was able to bring them home.

When Leanne told me that the NICU-world was her target market, I thought it fantastic, and told her so.

"I am your target market. I am your NICU parent."

I also told her that I wasn't convinced it would work.

She proved me wrong.

Leanne found nurses. She found other parents like me—with followings and lists—who do different types of marketing in the Parent market. She just started asking them to participate in her interviews.

Twelve people agreed, and while she was going through the process, two of her interviewees asked *her* to speak on their stages… *and they paid her for it.*

All of this happened before she added a single person to her email list.

After that, one of the nurses she spoke with—one with a following—happened to be putting together a course, and asked Leanne to help her with it. Even though, at that point, the nurse was the only one with a list to promote to, she offered Leanne a 50/50 split on the profits so long as she contributed half of the work it took to create it.

Strategic byproducts.

Once again, *all of this* happened before Leanne added a single person to her list.

When Leanne *did* begin promoting her Expert Showcase Series, her list-building efforts paid off, resulting in upwards of 200 people who subscribed within the first week. At this point, she has over four-to-five-hundred contacts now, and she's in a completely different space.

She's growing her business.

She's working with these nurses.

She's working with these families.

Her business has completely changed because of this.

The point is this: if it can work in the NICU market, it can work in any market.

YOUR ONE
QUESTION

YOUR ONE QUESTION

Let's finish with an exercise. This is how we come up with the one question that you're going to ask your experts.

Remember—as I said—your question can be one of either *aspiration or problem solving.*

Let's look a couple *aspirational* questions to consider:

- What is the single most important goal your prospects want to achieve?
- What are the burning questions and biggest goals that are most important to my prospects?

Now, let's look at *problem solving*. What's the most troubling problem your prospects want you to solve?

Your turn.

Make a list of possible interview questions. Do it with both methods in mind. Write down five different aspirational questions worth asking, and five potential problem solving questions. Then, *pick one*.

Whichever one you pick is the one you'll ask your experts and remember that *each of them is answering the same question.*

CONCLUSION

CONCLUSION

In conclusion, the Expert Showcase Series *will work for you*. I am confident that it truly is one of the best, simplest ways to build your list, establish partner relationships and grow your revenue.

It sure doesn't hurt to have the additional benefit of establishing yourself as an expert within your market, either—a feat that, as you've seen exemplified in the *Transfer of Authority* phenomenon thus far, is possible for anyone to accomplish.

No matter how often imposter syndrome rears its ugly head (and trust me… it comes for us all, regardless of our level of expertise), there's nothing to be afraid of.

I've done my best to give you relatable examples and easy-to-follow steps in an effort to provide you with the confident assurance that applying this method is every bit as easy as is learning about it.

For additional help—and as a means to that end—I recommend working through my accompanying guide, The *Expert Showcase Series: 10 Day List Building Challenge Workbook*, which will help you organize and successfully implement this process.

As I write this, I am many years removed from that fateful five minutes of stage-time in 2010, when I was given an expert's trust to help others grow their online businesses.

Here again, I want to thank *you* for giving me the opportunity to continue to teach others how to build their field of dreams…

I have no doubt that you will. Here's to your home run!

QUESTIONS

QUESTIONS

Q — Do you interview / post yourself among the video showcase, too, as an authority-build?

A — Yes. Absolutely. *You are one of the experts as part of this showcase series.* Why? Because you are now included in and elevated among your "peers" as an authority figure alongside these other experts. So, audiences see you on the same level as everyone else. Plus, you get to spread your message in your market about what you're doing. You absolutely include yourself as one of the interviews.

Q — Who interviews you, as the host / one elevating yourself to authority-figure status?

A — You could just answer your own question into a camera, or you could get somebody—maybe one of the other experts—to interview you. Either way works.

Q — When people opt in to this series, they are now on your list, right? Do you send a subsequent email to them that introduces what your regular email series is about, so that they know they're part of your list?

A — Yes. New subscribers should get your follow up sequence. The first email should remind them that they entered your email list and give them a link to go directly to the expert series. Of course, when they opted in—if you have your funnel set up correctly—they should have been immediately redirected to it. Additionally, though, the first email should be like a welcome email with a link back to the showcase also, so they remember where they came from.

Q — What do you use to film these experts? And how do you snip the beginning and end of your interview in order to make the final video presentable?

A — For recording: Zoom. Super simple. One screen. I try to make everything as *easy as possible*. I'm the "clarity" guy. Zoom. That's it.

For editing: Both Windows and Apple have free software that you can use. All you're cutting off is the banter at the beginning and end of your interview. Everything in the middle stays. Simply trim the ends, and you're done.

Q — How would you treat someone who doesn't have an opt-in list? For example: in my domain, which is basically disaster response and recovery, I might want to interview the administrator for FEMA—the Federal Emergency Management Agency. He's probably not building a list, but is of equal value and validity as me…?

A — In certain markets, I highly suggest including experts without lists. It's not *disadvantageous*, by any means. Again, this isn't all about list-building. It will boost up your expert series, regardless. For example: of the ten people on your "panel," perhaps eight of them have lists, but the two who don't are nevertheless of high importance and great authority—much like the FEMA administrator. It's *great to simply have them involved*, and others will be impressed by who they are, regardless. Like, "Woah, you've got the director of FEMA right there. This is awesome!"

Does that make sense? It pays off to include people without lists, you just have to be a bit strategic about it.

Q — Do you give the participants first right of refusal? Do you let them see the interview and decide whether they actually want to?

A — Yeah, I do. I let them see the interview. But here's the thing: remember that—in many ways—this is a numbers' game.

In the beginning, I showed you how to do a search and I told you to find 50 to 100 experts. Google, Facebook, and Amazon..

Now you have a list of 100 people, and out of those hundred, you're only going to get a certain amount of people that are going to actually say yes, and do it with you. Let's say it's 20. Right, so we got 100, we're down to 20. It's a numbers game.

Same thing when you're ready to promote. When you're ready to promote—even though all 20 said *"I'll do it for you…"*— they're not going to.

It's just a fact. They're not going to.

Just like when we do a Joint Venture promotion and they say they're going to promote… they don't. It's the same thing, and it's okay. Really, you only *need* two or three of them to promote to their list. When that happens, you'll watch as two-to-three-hundred people join your list in the snap of a finger. It'd be great, but you don't need all twenty. You just need a few to get a list build.

Q — You said to ask the same question of everyone. Does it *have to be* the same question?

A — No, it doesn't have to be. I'm just trying to make it simple. That said, I think it's advantageous, because people *do* like to see the same question answered by different experts. There's a wide array of perspectives on how to handle any given question. They'd like to see what *Expert A* has to say about the same thing as *Expert B.*

Q — You mentioned something about *repeating* the process. Do you mean that we should add new interviews to the already-existing page, or start out from scratch all over again?

A — Let's say you have ten interviews on your page. Three months after your initial push, you can add another five expert interviews to that same page, and bring in new traffic from *just those five, new partners.* This time, new traffic will see all fifteen interviews, instead of just the ten, which is why it's replicable and you can keep doing it over and over again.

Q — How do you make sure that the content you receive from your expert is actually educational, and not just a sales pitch?

A — The expert is simply answering the question you're asking them, and ultimately it is your choice about whether or not to include it. Because these are pre-recorded interviews, if you don't like it, don't post it. Online summits tend to be live-streams, but these video-responses aren't.

When you set up the interview, you definitely—in the email instructions—tell them exactly what you're wanting. (And it's usually on a zoom call, because you can get it recorded while it's happening.) They know the question ahead of time. They're answering it for 10 minutes. And then you just take that content and embed it in the funnel I've shown you.

Q — I have a tangible-goods business. My family has a screen printing business and we make a calendar. I want to sell more. Every year, we grow a little bit. Last year, in May, we sold two-thousand calendars. This year, I want to sell three-thousand calendars. Can you give me some ideas about who I should be interviewing? We have an 85% return customer rate, which is awesome. Most of our buyers are creative people who appreciate handmade things, which consists of two demographics: older and younger. The younger demographic is generally made up of hipster people who are appreciative of handmade goods in an age where they're not that common, and that's who I'd like to target.

A— Great. So, you look at who is buying the calendars. There are many different directions you *can* go, but consider this: look up handcrafted magazines and find out which of them are at the top. Research experts and influencers in crafts then start interviewing them. We don't have to do a deep-dive into a specific niche here. We just get a bunch of craftspeople.

Now, because of that, your list isn't going to be super targeted, and we might need to work on cleaning the list a little bit after you have it. But again, the main point of *this particular strategy is relationship-building…*

Imagine relationships with these craftspeople who have influence in your market. Let's say you've got ten new partners and you're ready to promote your product. What do you do? You go back to those ten people and ask, *"Do you want to work on this deal together?"* Right? I know we keep thinking about lists, but in your case, I'm thinking about relationships.

POSTSCRIPT

POSTSCRIPT

I'm excited for you and your business, and each and every new opportunity the Expert Showcase Series will bring. Please send me updates on your small wins along the way!

Marc@ZaZoMarketing.com

Speaking of opportunities, I know that—sometimes—more in-depth, step-by-step provisions are necessary to help guide people through what can feel like a daunting process.

If that is the case—if that's how you're feeling—I'd like to invite you to join me in either my Online List building Coaching Program, or my *4-Week Online List Building Workshop.*

The coaching program welcomes guests into a step-by-step course, complete with video tutorials, worksheets and real-life examples throughout.

The workshop is a bit more of a hands-on experience wherein we walk through the process together, live, over the course of a four-week period. Each week, you'll work through a specific part of the process, and we'll meet so that I can answer any questions and help you break through potential roadblocks before beginning on the following week's coursework.

If you are interested in this program, just click the link below. The first offer is for the coaching program, and if you join, you will be offered to upgrade to the workshop if you so choose.

https://www.ExpertShowcaseSeries.com/Coaching

No matter what, I look forward to working with you and hearing about your great results.

Marc Evans

www.ingramcontent.com/pod-product-compliance
Lightning Source LLC
Chambersburg PA
CBHW080423240526
45472CB00022B/2222